ECHOES OF SUCCESS

CASE STUDIES IN THE REPLICATION OF
ASIAN DEVELOPMENT BANK PROJECTS
IN THE PEOPLE'S REPUBLIC OF CHINA

SEPTEMBER 2024

ADB

ASIAN DEVELOPMENT BANK

Notes:
In this publication, "$" refers to United States dollars and "CNY" refers to yuan.
ADB recognizes "China" as the People's Republic of China.

Cover design by Maria Azel Cabello Gorne.

CONTENTS

▶ Foreword

The pace and scale of development progress in the People's Republic of China (PRC) over the past 40 years has been remarkable. Since the 1980s, a sustained period of high economic growth has made the PRC the world's second-largest economy. It has also generated gains in poverty reduction without historical precedent. In just 4 decades, 850 million people have emerged from poverty. And as of 2020, the country has eradicated extreme poverty in its population of 1.4 billion people.

Undoubtedly, other countries in Asia and the Pacific would do well to better understand the PRC's development progress as they chart their own growth paths. Indeed, the Chinese themselves have been eager to impart lessons learned under the banner of South–South cooperation.

Alongside such efforts, the Asian Development Bank (ADB) has sought to share its experiences as one of the PRC's key development partners from the time the country joined the bank in 1986. Working with national and provincial governments over a 40-year period, ADB has pursued projects in the PRC across a wide range of sectors and, along the way, has helped to strengthen policies and institutional capacity in support of development objectives.

In recent years, ADB's partnership with the PRC has focused on mitigating the environmental costs of a high-growth economy. This has included local and regional efforts to improve air quality and preserve biodiversity. But the largest objective by far has been to accelerate the shift toward a green economy. As the world's largest source of annual carbon dioxide emissions, the PRC is now intensively engaged in efforts to reorient from a carbon-intensive model of development to one that decouples economic growth from carbon dioxide emissions.

Accelerating the green transition within the PRC is a global climate imperative, but it also represents an opportunity to demonstrate new models for development across Asia and the Pacific. As a result, ADB's focus in the PRC is shifting to areas where it can add value through innovative demonstration projects that generate regional public goods, knowledge, and best practices for replication, particularly when it comes to climate mitigation and resilience in the face of climate change. The PRC, with its robust project preparation and implementation capacity, offers particularly fertile ground for extracting valuable lessons from successful ADB operations that can be applied elsewhere.

This publication assembles five case studies in the demonstration and replication of ADB-financed projects in the PRC. The quintet of case studies spans diverse themes, reflecting the breadth and depth of ADB's country program in the PRC in recent years. From green finance to nature conservation to urban greening, each case study illuminates a unique facet of development showcasing how private funding can be crowded in, a wetlands ecosystem is restored, rare species are repopulated, and an urban waste and water system is rehabilitated.

Although there is no single formula for success, key factors facilitating replication include alignment with government strategies and priorities, and knowledge-sharing among ADB project officers and consultants as well as local government officials and project management offices in the PRC.

These case studies provide valuable insights into key elements of successful demonstration and replication. I hope this publication inspires other institutions to increase their development impacts, both within the PRC and in other developing member countries. In the process, I also look forward to its contribution to the global pool of knowledge on development issues.

Scott Allen Morris
Vice-President
East and Southeast Asia, and the Pacific
Asian Development Bank

▶ Acknowledgments

These cases were prepared by the study team of the East Asia Department (EARD) of the Asian Development Bank (ADB). The team was composed of Marzia Mongiorgi, former principal economist, EARD (until June 2023), Hsiao Chink Tang, senior economist; Bart Édes, who drafted the cases; and Marga Domingo-Morales, who provided research and coordination support. Kelly Bird, advisor from EARD, provided guidance to this publication. Safdar Parvez, country director, People's Republic of China (PRC) Resident Mission, and Lee Ming Tai, unit head of portfolio management, offered valuable guidance on case study selection.

Dozens of officials of project management offices (PMOs), executing agencies, and central and subnational governments in the PRC, and ADB project team leaders generously provided their time, inputs, and thoughtful perspectives vital to the selection and elaboration of the case studies. Special thanks are due to Guo Biao and Zhan Shu, directors in the International Financial Institution Division II of the Department of International Economic and Financial Cooperation in the PRC Ministry of Finance, for their invaluable guidance and support to this initiative.

ADB staff members Duncan Lang and Niu Zhiming shared valuable perspectives and context that were essential in preparing the case on A Biodiversity Protection Project in the People's Republic of China Helps Lift an Ambitious Regional Initiative.

The case on Scaling Private Investment in the Green Economy drew upon information provided by CICC Capital Management Company Limited, a subsidiary of China International Capital Corporation Limited (CICC), as well as ADB staff members Kang Hang Leung, Benita Ainabe, Abhishek Hegde, Anouj Mehta, and Naeeda Crishna Morgado.

The case on Saving Lives on Asia's Roads relied heavily on inputs provided by ADB staff members Rebecca Stapleton and Xia Heng.

The Shaanxi Financial Holdings Group Development and Investment Management Company provided helpful inputs for the case on Catalyzing Finance for Energy Efficiency and Renewables, and ADB staff member Gloria Gerilla-Teknomo extended her support to the elaboration of this part of the publication.

The case on Improving the Urban Environment through Integrated Water Resources Management benefited from information provided by a variety of local government authorities in the PRC, including representatives of the PMOs of the Wuhan Urban Environmental Improvement Project, Hubei Huangshi Urban Pollution Control Environmental Management Project, and Anhui Huainan Urban Water Systems Integrated Rehabilitation Project, as well as municipal officials from Huainan and Huangshi. ADB staff member Baochang Zheng greatly assisted in the preparation of this case.

Through the ADB-PRC Regional Knowledge Sharing Initiative (RKSI), Hsiao Chink Tang and Dan Wang captured footages from the field, and shared them on the RKSI website. RKSI also organized a project sharing session of these cases at the second East Asia Forum held in Changsha, PRC in October 2023.

Siyang Liu capably coordinated project site visits and meetings with government and project authorities in the PRC. Maria Theresa Mercado edited the cases and Maria Azel Gorne did the layout and design. Lou Andrea Cabanilla extended reliable administrative support throughout the preparation of the publication.

► Abbreviations

ACGF	ASEAN Catalytic Green Finance Facility
ADB	Asian Development Bank
AFD	Agence Française de Développement
AIF	ASEAN Infrastructure Fund
ASEAN	Association of Southeast Asian Nations
CO$_2$	carbon dioxide
EAAF	East Asian–Australasian Flyway
iRAP	International Road Assessment Programme
km	kilometer
m^3	cubic meter
PRC	People's Republic of China
RFI	Regional Flyway Initiative
SDG	Sustainable Development Goal
SGDF	Shandong Green Development Fund
SMEs	small and medium-sized enterprises
TA	technical assistance
UNESCO	United Nations Educational, Scientific and Cultural Organization

▶ Introduction

Across the vast landscape of development projects, the People's Republic of China (PRC) stands out as a formidable canvas, offering a rich tapestry of opportunities for learning and replication—to be applied to other projects both domestically and abroad.

Replication occurs when the design, or a unique feature of a project, is adopted by another project—either in the country or another country. For the Asian Development Bank (ADB), an operation must be designed to showcase some distinctive new feature or approach for its replication. The features can vary and might include, for example, a unique funding mechanism, a detailed methodology, an engineering or design feature, the structural setup for a new institution, or even an entire project design.

In 2019, ADB carried out a study to determine what part such replication has played in its operations in the PRC. A total of 22 ADB-financed projects in the country were examined. The study revealed that about half of the projects were replicated—especially those that focused on environment and climate change management. This initial research helped to inform the further development of ADB's tailored approach to upper middle-income countries under its Strategy 2030.

In an update to the 2019 work, ADB's East Asia Department in 2022 examined additional ADB-financed projects in the PRC. For this exercise, the study team looked at ADB project documents, interviewed ADB staff, consulted with government counterparts and project management officials, and carried out site visits.

From this work, five case studies were compiled to showcase replication within the PRC and/or other developing member countries. These were presented at the East Asia Forum in Changsha, Hunan Province, PRC, in October 2023. These case studies form the substance of this publication.

The five projects address diverse areas—nature conservation, green finance, urban development, energy efficiency and environmental improvement, and road safety.

The Jiangsu Yancheng Biodiversity Protection Project illustrates the practical application of eco-compensation to mitigate development impacts on biodiversity and ecosystem services. It emphasizes the importance of institutional strengthening and effective coordination among public sector bodies. The lessons learned in nurturing coexistence between threatened species and humans have been applied to adjacent areas by local Chinese authorities. The project's significance transcends borders, contributing to the protection and sustainable management of the East Asian–Australasian Flyway —a remarkable Asian conservation story.

The Shandong Green Development Fund is an innovative funding mechanism that leverages public funds to mobilize substantial private, institutional, and commercial investment, focused on advancing the Sustainable Development Goals with a climate and environmental lens. It has stimulated similar funds in Southeast Asia and sparked interest in green development financing in Central and West Asia.

The Shaanxi Mountain Road Safety Demonstration Project in northwestern PRC inspired the replication of the International Road Assessment Programme road safety

methodology to Hunan, Heilongjiang, and even Mongolia, showcasing the project's ability to go beyond geographical boundaries and promote road safety through a practical participatory approach.

Meanwhile, the Shaanxi Accelerated Energy Efficiency and Environment Improvement Financing Project is a catalyst for reduced energy intensity and emissions in Shaanxi Province. Its success has contributed to a substantial increase in the share of renewable energy sources in the province's power supply, overcoming financing barriers and leveraging significant investments for clean energy. The project is being replicated in neighboring Henan Province.

The Wuhan Urban Environmental Improvement Project marks a pioneering stride in comprehensive sludge management, circular economy promotion, and climate change mitigation. Its innovative design has created a model that extends beyond its initial scope, influencing lake rehabilitation, integrated surface water management, and flood management in Wuhan, across Hubei Province, and beyond.

These case studies underscore the versatility and adaptability of the lessons learned. The PRC's commitment to incorporating successful methodologies into its broader development agenda has served as a driving force for the replication of these projects. The country will continue to be a key contributor to the development of regional and global public goods as it plays a pivotal role in disseminating best practices and fostering a culture of continuous improvement.

A Biodiversity Protection Project in the People's Republic of China Helps Lift an Ambitious Regional Initiative

Flocks of birds soar along the East Asian–Australasian Flyway (EAAF) as they migrate thousands of kilometers between their breeding grounds and the places where they pass the winter. The migratory path that constitutes the flyway reaches from Alaska and the Far North of the Russian Federation to the southern parts of Australia and New Zealand. The EAAF includes large parts of East Asia and Southeast Asia, as well as Bangladesh and the Andaman and Nicobar Islands. Intensive development activities such as rapid urbanization, land use change, and coastal reclamation threaten the intertidal and inland wetlands upon which migratory birds rely. The numbers of some species, like the spoon-billed sandpiper, have steadily declined over the past few decades and are now at critically low levels.

The spoon-billed sandpiper breeds in a small area of northeast Russia. In autumn, it wings along Asia's Pacific coast, refueling at traditional stopover sites in various countries, eventually migrating 8,000 kilometers (km) to reach its winter haunts in Bangladesh, Thailand, Myanmar, Viet Nam, and southern parts of the People's Republic of China (PRC). Today, only 773 of these birds remain (490 being breeding adults).[1] Habitat loss due to tidal flat reclamation along its migratory route remains a grave threat to the spoon-billed sandpiper's survival.

Threats to Migratory Birds

Migration is one of the most remarkable aspects of birds' lives. Many species migrate along eight broadly well-established routes known as flyways. The EAAF extends across the territory of many members of ADB. More than 50 million migratory waterbirds of more than 210 species—along with many other animal and plant species—depend on thousands of the flyway's wetlands for food, shelter, and other essential needs. Wetlands support livelihoods with food and clean water and opportunities in re-creation and tourism. They also deliver flood regulating services, sequester carbon, and assist with climate change adaptation and resilience.[2]

Asia's rapid economic development has exacted a substantial toll on the environment, negatively impacting many key wetland sites and species. Fifty species that use EAAF are currently considered at risk of global extinction.

Protecting Wetlands While Supporting Local Livelihoods

International cooperation and coordination are required to overcome the many threats to migratory birds along the length of the flyway. Without coordinated actions, efforts

[1] J. Lowen. 2022. *Fewer than 500 Left: Why Saving Spoonie is a Race Against Time.* BirdLife International. 6 May.
[2] ADB. 2020. The East Asian-Australasian Flyway – Opportunities to Support Wetlands, Livelihoods, and Biodiversity in East and Southeast Asia. Webinar. 16 October.

Protecting migratory waterbirds and their habitats. Migratory birds like the spoon-billed sandpiper and bar-tailed godwit rely on wetlands for food and shelter needs *(photo by Ge Naihang)*.

in individual countries will not solve the multiple threats to the network of wetlands and so cooperative efforts are needed to identify, protect, and sustainably manage key sites for migratory waterbirds across borders. An excellent example of such efforts may be found in the Yancheng coastal wetlands of Jiangsu Province in the PRC, which is a key site for many species using the flyway.

ADB's Jiangsu Yancheng Wetlands Protection Project[3] covers an extensive area within the Yancheng coastal wetlands of Jiangsu Province. This area is renowned as the world's largest intertidal wetland system and lies along the EAAF. Hosting over 400 bird species, 29 of which are endangered, the wetland system spans two national nature reserves and two forest farms within the project zone.

The Yancheng Rare Birds National Nature Reserve, one of the nature reserves, provides the principal winter habitat for 40%–80% of the worldwide population of the red-crowned crane, an endangered species. Another national nature reserve, Dafeng Milu, shelters the Père David's Deer (*Elaphurus davidianus*), which is extinct in its natural habitat. Both reserves are listed on the Ramsar Convention's List of Wetlands of International Importance, acknowledging the distinctiveness of their wetland ecosystems and the biodiversity of their species.

Apart from their biodiversity importance, the Yancheng wetlands deliver crucial ecosystem services to nearby communities. Local livelihoods rely on harvesting and cultivating marine and estuarine plants and fish species. Furthermore, these wetlands serve as a buffer against coastal erosion, tsunamis, and storm surges while enhancing water quality by absorbing certain pollutants originating from households, industries, and agriculture.

The two national nature reserves and two forest farms draw significant tourist traffic, creating job opportunities and income for the surrounding communities. This intertwining of ecological services with economic development has contributed to poverty reduction and improved the livelihoods of local populations.

---

[3] ADB. 2011. *Report and Recommendation of the President to the Board of Directors: Proposed Loan to the People's Republic of China for the Jiangsu Yancheng Wetlands Protection Project.* ADB. 2020. *Completion Report: Jiangsu Yancheng Wetlands Protection Project in the People's Republic of China.*

The wetlands served by the project fall under the PRC Biodiversity Conservation Strategy and Action Plan, spanning from 2011 to 2030. The nature reserves are integral to the national implementation plan for wetland preservation, and the wetlands hold priority status in Jiangsu provincial wetland protection plans. Employing an integrated strategy, the project aimed to tackle challenges associated with wetland conservation by applying engineering measures as well as policy actions and social development interventions. The Government of the PRC financed more than half ($30.5 million) of the actual project cost of $57.7 million, while ADB's actual funding was $25.8 million. In addition, the Global Environment Facility provided a $1.4 million grant.

Inspiring Biodiversity Protection Beyond the Project

Approved by ADB in 2011, the Jiangsu Yancheng Biodiversity Protection Project supported the restoration or rehabilitation of more than 4,500 hectares (ha) of wetlands, providing healthy habitats for many bird and animal species. Infrastructure and management facilities were substantially improved in the two national nature reserves and surrounding forest farms, and the wetland bird population within the Rare Bird Nature core zone increased by 365% during the life of the project.

The project also contributed to strengthening of the institutional capacity for wetlands protection and habitats management, assisted the Jiangsu provincial government in developing a policy framework on eco-compensation, and provided training to local communities in biodiversity conservation techniques. The project played a key role in the registration of the Yancheng wetlands on the United Nations Educational, Scientific and Cultural Organization (UNESCO) World Heritage List in 2019.

The Jiangsu provincial government was responsible for oversight and coordination among various agencies, such as those responsible for ecology and environment, finance, and forestry; water resource departments and bureaus; and the Jiangsu Provincial Development and Reform Commission.

Various project measures and approaches have been replicated in government-funded wetland protection activities. Certain physical features, like protective fencing, were adopted

Wetland rehabilitation in Jiangsu Province. Oriental stork in nestling, one of the world's rarest bird species found in the Yancheng wetlands *(photo by Chen Guoyuan).*

in surrounding forested areas managed by private enterprises and villages. For instance, the project's eco-compensation scheme, which is used to protect endangered deer and people's livelihoods, was replicated by Dafeng District. The Jiangsu Yancheng Biodiversity Protection Project has raised awareness of biodiversity conservation domestically and internationally through its exhibition center, staffed by trained tour guides.

Aspects of the project are currently being integrated into a proposed ADB-funded project geared toward the ecological revitalization and climate-resilient advancement of South Dongting Lake. This proposed project seeks to rejuvenate wetlands and freshwater ecosystems by implementing comprehensive climate resilience measures and landscape planning. Situated in the southwest region of Dongting Lake, South Dongting Lake is important to maintaining climate regulation and ecological stability in the middle and lower segments of the Yangtze River. In addition, it delivers essential ecosystem services to local inhabitants, including soil fertility, potable water, freshwater for agricultural use, and navigable water routes.

The planned project will utilize aspects from the Jiangsu Yancheng Biodiversity Protection Project and other ADB operations, including: (i) eco-compensation programs aimed at encouraging the adoption of eco-farming and wetland-friendly farming practices through a landscape-focused approach, (ii) strengthening institutions and enhancing interagency coordination to ensure comprehensive protection of wetland and freshwater ecosystems across the basin, (iii) employing nature-based solutions for both conservation and restoration efforts, and (iv) creating incentive structures to encourage private sector investment in low-carbon and climate-resilient solutions.

Looking beyond the borders of the PRC, the Jiangsu Yancheng Biodiversity Protection Project played an indispensable catalytic role in the launch of the ADB Regional Flyway Initiative (RFI), which was set up to protect wetlands across many countries. The successful implementation and demonstrated impacts of the project, together with the credibility bestowed by UNESCO recognition, encouraged ADB to think bigger and create the RFI in October 2021.

The RFI, established with the East Asian–Australasian Flyway Partnership Secretariat and BirdLife International, has the goal to mobilize finance with partners to invest $3 billion in protection and sustainable management of priority wetlands along the flyway. Plans for the RFI include development of a long-term programmatic approach to invest in projects to protect and restore EAAF wetland ecosystems and the services they provide over the next 10 plus years (Box 1.1).

A Catalyst for Broader Conservation Efforts

The ADB-financed Jiangsu Yancheng Biodiversity Protection Project was a groundbreaking intervention. It demonstrated the practical use of eco-compensation to mitigate the impacts of development on biodiversity and ecosystem services and highlighted the importance of institutional strengthening and effective coordination among public sector bodies. Learnings from the project on how to nurture coexistence between threatened species and humans have been applied to geographically adjacent areas by local Chinese authorities. Further, the project has directly and indirectly paved the way to scale up ambition for biodiversity initiatives in the PRC that will contribute to the protection and sustainable management of EAAF, which is emerging as one of the great Asian conservation stories of its time.

BOX 1.1
The ADB Regional Flyway Initiative

As the Asian Development Bank (ADB) has raised its ambitions on climate change and nature, investing in wetlands through the Regional Flyway Initiative (RFI) provides an ideal platform to achieve a scale that can make a regional impact. RFI will give special attention to migratory waterbirds since they depend on wetlands along the flyway. In addition, migratory waterbirds capture the public's imagination, which will be important to generate support for protecting and sustainably managing the wetlands over the long term.

The RFI blueprint involves devising a comprehensive, long-term strategy to invest in projects aimed at safeguarding and revitalizing East Asian-Australasian Flyway (EAAF) wetland ecosystems and their associated services for the next decade and beyond.

Five indicative project models have been developed to enhance understanding around what an individual project might look like and to display investment viability: (i) habitat restoration and protection, (ii) sustainable aquaculture and fisheries, (iii) sustainable agriculture, (iv) pollution prevention and water management, and (v) nature protection and eco-tourism.

RFI projects will likely be a mix of these models, and climate adaptation and mitigation will cut across all of them. Solutions will be tailored to every site and interested ADB developing member countries (DMCs) or project owners can develop projects based on their priorities and considerations.

ADB is supporting the RFI through a $1.7 million technical assistance (TA) grant. The ADB-managed Regional Cooperation and Integration Fund, financed by the Government of Japan, is providing 80% of the TA funding.

The TA project has identified wetland sites of international importance to migratory waterbirds. ADB is now consulting with governments, partners, and stakeholders to produce a final list of priority sites from which 50 investment concepts will be developed. Work is underway to identify capacity issues among participating governments, and to create a financing mechanism to mobilize funding, particularly from EAAF Partnership members that are also members of ADB.

Consultations and knowledge exchange under the TA are ongoing through existing forums, such as the 14th Conference of the Contracting Parties of the Convention on Wetlands (Ramsar Convention) in 2022, the 11th Meeting of the Partners of the EAAF Partnership in 2023, and the recent country-level consultation in the Philippines.

The following 10 economies are participating in the RFI: Bangladesh, Cambodia, the People's Republic of China, Indonesia, Lao People's Democratic Republic (Lao PDR), Malaysia, Mongolia, Philippines, Thailand, and Viet Nam. These economies were selected because of their status as ADB DMCs, as well as their geographic location within the flyway, the importance of their wetlands, and their membership (all but Lao PDR) in the EAAF Partnership.

Sources: ADB. 2021. ADB, Multilateral Banks Commit to Mainstreaming Nature at COP26. News Release. 2 November; ADB. 2021. *Technical Assistance for Scaling Up the East Asian-Australasian Flyway Initiative.*

Scaling Private Investment in the Green Economy

The Asia and Pacific region needs to invest $1.5 trillion annually to achieve the Sustainable Development Goals (SDGs) by 2030.[4] The public sector can only fill part of the massive gap that exists between current funding and actual financing needed to tackle problems like pollution, environmental degradation, threats to biodiversity, and climate change. Public institutions, from the municipal level up to multilateral institutions like ADB, can play a critical role in stimulating private investment in activities that support a sustainable economy.

Together with partners in the PRC, ADB launched a financing platform that has been replicated in Southeast Asia, marshaling substantial capital in support of the SDGs —such as SDG 13, which aims to limit and adapt to climate change—as well as addressing environmental degradation, threats to biodiversity, and unsustainable consumption of natural resources. The origins of the innovative Chinese platform can be traced back to important knowledge work carried out by ADB staff.

From Knowledge to Action

In 2017, ADB published Catalyzing Green Finance: A Concept for Leveraging Blended Finance for Green Development. The report proposed a conceptual approach to establishing a "green finance catalyzing facility" capable of attracting substantial private sector finance into green projects.

Such a facility would provide a model that could be used to create a larger green finance system for a country.

This facility uses concessional finance to mitigate project risks and costs while allocating risks to participating parties best suited to manage them. Funding depended on the development of road maps and the meeting of green policy objectives. In this manner, a green finance catalyzing facility marries financial sustainability with environmental sustainability.

ADB soon put this concept into practice in the PRC. In 2019, ADB approved financing for the Shandong Green Development Fund Project (SGDF), a multitiered fund that aims to address negative impacts of climate change. The SGDF intends to make at least 70% of its investments in Shandong Province, and is designed to create a pipeline of sustainable and replicable subprojects aligned with a set of climate assessment guidelines. All investments are screened with criteria set under these guidelines, which are based on the Green Climate Fund Investment Framework.[5]

The SGDF's investment portfolio comprises climate mitigation and adaptation subprojects assessed against eligibility criteria intended to facilitate Shandong's shift to a low-carbon, climate-resilient development path. The SGDF features a 20-year catalytic fund that has received seed capital from bilateral and

---

4 Shu Tian, et al. 2021. Filling the Finance Gap for a Green and Inclusive Recovery. ADB Blogs. 10 June.
5 Green Climate Fund.

Financing climate-positive investment. The operation of logistics electric vehicles will reduce air pollutant and carbon dioxide emissions, and the use of fuel in Shandong Province *(photo by Shandong Green Development Fund)*.

multilateral development agencies. These funds are then blended with capital from private, institutional, and commercial sources and then channeled into a series of operating funds for investments in climate-positive subprojects.

The inaugural SGDF operating fund, SGDF I, was set up in 2021 and has raised CNY716 million, or the equivalent of just under $100 million. ADB, Agence Française de Développement (AFD), and KfW Development Bank have provided CNY408 million (about $56 million) to SGDF I. Other investors, including the Qingdao municipal government, have provided the remaining balance.

In 2022, SGDF I invested in two climate-positive subprojects: an electric vehicle logistics service, and an energy and electric vehicle charging internet platform. More than 25,000 logistics electric vehicles have been purchased under the first subproject, and more than 45,000 electric vehicle charging stations have been connected by the second.

A second operating fund, SGDF II, is expected to start operating by the end of

2024. SGDF II, which is to be registered in Jinan City, the capital of Shandong Province, will have a targeted fund size of about CNY3.3 billion (about $456 million). The Jinan municipal government has invested in the fund.

A third operating fund, SGDF III, has been launched in collaboration with the municipal government of Weihai, a coastal city in Shandong Province. This fund, registered in December 2022 and created with funding of around CNY500 million (about $69 million), has started operations since 2023.

Lessons Adopted in Southeast Asia

SGDF has not only stimulated the establishment of multiple funds in the PRC, but also informed the establishment of the ASEAN Catalytic Green Finance Facility (ACGF). Set up in 2019, the ACGF is an initiative of the ASEAN Infrastructure Fund (AIF). ADB staff who prepared the ACGF regularly cited the example of the SGDF with prospective partners and investors to highlight the potential of a Southeast Asian facility that would finance environmentally sustainable, low-carbon, climate-resilient projects (Box 2.1).

BOX 2.1

A Financing Boost for the Sustainable Development Goals in Indonesia

Drawing on the experience of the previously mentioned green financing initiatives in Shandong Province and Southeast Asia, the Asian Development Bank (ADB) approved a $150 million financial intermediation loan to the Government of Indonesia in February 2022 to enable the implementation of Phase 1 of the Sustainable Development Goals Indonesia One-Green Finance Facility (SIO-GFF). The government subsequently on-lent the borrowed funds to the SIO-GFF financial intermediary, PT Sarana Multi Infrastruktur (Persero) (PT SMI), a state-owned infrastructure financing institution. ADB's $150 million financing has the potential to mobilize an investment pool of up to $1.13 billion for about 20 green and Sustainable Development Goal (SDG)-driven projects within the SIO-GFF framework. This demonstrates a multiplier effect of nearly eight times, showcasing the substantial leverage of ADB financing in stimulating investments.

ADB contributed to the elaboration of green and SDG screening frameworks to support the establishment of SIO-GFF. It has also undertaken feasibility studies of pipeline projects, and is now helping PT SMI explore opportunities for mobilizing subsequent financing from other development partners interested in participating in SIO-GFF. Further, ADB has shared global best practices in innovative and leveraged finance and and its knowledge of green finance as a crosscutting theme across many of the SDGs. The SIO-GFF supports the achievement of Indonesia's commitments to climate change and the SDGs by financing eligible subprojects that meet green, financial bankability, and leverage targets with the aim of catalyzing additional funds from private, institutional, and commercial sources. The facility will support greenfield subprojects during periods of high credit risk, such as the construction phase, and the early years of commercial operations when cash flow is typically negative. For green subprojects, at least 30% of the mobilized financing must be provided by private, institutional, and commercial sources.

The SIO-GFF aids Indonesia in fulfilling its pledges on climate change and the Global Goals by funding qualified subprojects that satisfy criteria for environmental sustainability, financial viability, and leveraging potential. The facility supports greenfield initiatives, particularly during phases of heightened credit risk, like construction, and initial operational years when cash flow tends to be negative. In the case of green projects, a minimum of 30% of the raised financing must originate from private, institutional, and commercial entities.

In December 2022, the first disbursement of SIO-GFF funds was made—$10 million for the Dumai Drinking Water Supply System Provision project. This project will improve service performance and expand the scope of piping for drinking water for more than 20,000 subscription connections in four subdistricts of Dumai, a coastal city in Riau province on the island of Sumatra. The project has been designed with a build–operate–transfer structure. In addition, PT SMI has committed to investing several additional projects to support the development of renewable energy, including solar photovoltaic and mini hydro.

Source: ADB. 2022. *Report and Recommendation from the President to the Board of Directors: Proposed Loan and Administration of Technical Assistance Grant to the Republic of Indonesia for the Sustainable Development Goals Indonesia One–Green Finance Facility (Phase 1).*

Supporting climate change mitigation. A subproject will upgrade and facilitate the development of electric vehicles—reducing emissions and improving the climate resilience of the transportation sector in Shandong Province (*photo by Shandong Green Development Fund*).

Private sector financiers are wary of investing in green infrastructure projects in Southeast Asia as they often entail large initial costs and are perceived as high-risk. Public financing is inadequate to meet the region's massive need for investment. The ACGF provides the region with access to green finance to help fill the substantial financing gap.

Since its launch in 2019, the ACGF has made available $1.9 billion in cofinancing and funds for technical assistance (TA) from nine financing partners,[6] including approximately $500 million in concessional funds to be channeled through ADB trust funds. The ACGF TA assists governments in preparing green infrastructure projects, while loans from the fund cover upfront capital investment costs. This two-pronged approach helps to reduce or reallocate risks in a way that makes a project more enticing to private investors.

Eligible ACGF projects must be sovereign or sovereign-guaranteed and have a proper financial sustainability plan. In addition, they are obligated to have clear environmental goals and targets and a road map for attracting private capital investment. The ACGF Investment Principles and Eligibility Criteria describe the requirements for project financing. Projects promoting sustainable urban transport, waste management, renewable energy, energy efficiency, water supply and sanitation, and climate-resilient agriculture are the focus of the ACGF.

The ACGF also offers knowledge services and training programs to build the institutional capacity of Association of Southeast Asian Nations (ASEAN) governments to scale up green infrastructure investments and provide upstream support to strengthen the regulatory environment.

During the first 5 years of ACGF operations (2019–2023), seven projects have been cofinanced by AIF and/or ACGF partners, representing $4.8 billion in total project cost, including $80 million from the AIF, $2.4 billion from ADB, and $1.1 billion earmarked to be financed by six ACGF partners. Approximately 73% of the project cost counts toward climate finance. Together, the projects are estimated to result in the reduction of an estimated 3 million tons of carbon dioxide equivalent (tCO_2e) per year. By the end of 2023, ADB had approved five of these projects.

---

[6] AFD, Cassa Depositi e Prestiti, European Investment Bank, European Union, Green Climate Fund, KfW, the Government of the Republic of Korea, and the Government of the United Kingdom.

Today, the ACGF serves as a one-stop-shop to identify, develop, and finance green projects in Southeast Asia, supporting the ASEAN governments in their efforts to meet their nationally determined contributions under the Paris Agreement and achieve their SDGs.

Seeding Green Finance Initiatives Across Asia

ADB is Asia's Climate Bank, having announced a commitment to marshal $100 billion in climate finance in developing Asia and the Pacific by 2030. To achieve this ambitious target, ADB and its partners have launched several initiatives to support climate change mitigation and adaptation activities and assist developing member countries in making their economies more environmentally sustainable.

The PRC has proved to be a fertile testing ground for an innovative platform that employs public funds to mobilize substantial private, institutional, and commercial investment in projects to advance the SDGs, including goals with a climate and environmental focus. Features and approaches of SGDF have been replicated in other funds in Southeast Asia and have stimulated the exploration of opportunities to expand green development financing in Central and West Asia (Box 2.2).

BOX 2.2

Nurturing Green Investment in Central and West Asia

The geographic range of the Shandong Green Development Fund (SGDF) project's potential replication has expanded westward across Asia. In 2022, the Asian Development Bank (ADB) approved a regional technical assistance (TA) for Enabling Green Recovery in Central and West Asia through a Sustainable Financing Program. Countries initially covered by the TA include Armenia, Kazakhstan, Pakistan, and Uzbekistan. The country coverage scope will be reviewed and may be expanded during the implementation of the TA, which has a budget of $1.92 million.

One output of the TA is helping selected countries develop a road map for establishing a national blended financing facility. Such a facility, modeled on the SGDF and subsequent ADB-backed facilities, would help estimate likely green targets delivered by financed projects, improve their bankability, and facilitate asset securitization by aggregating smaller high-potential sustainable infrastructure projects. The facility would pool sovereign, multilateral, bilateral, and international financial institution resources and leverage sovereign funds to catalyze additional private institutional capital.

Source: ADB. 2022. *Technical Assistance for Enabling Green Recovery in Central and West Asia through a Sustainable Financing Program.*

Saving Lives on Asia's Roads

The road traffic fatality rate in the PRC stands at 18.8 per 100,000 population[7]—higher than those of many other countries in the Asia and Pacific region, and higher than those of most other countries with large economies. The World Bank estimates that road crashes cost the PRC 6.2% of its gross domestic product.

ADB has supported the PRC in its efforts to further improve road safety. An example is the Shaanxi Mountain Road Safety Demonstration Project in the northwestern part of the country. The project's geographic area, encompassing Xunyang County, Hanbin District, and Shangnan County, including prefecture cities of Ankang and Shangluo, hosts a multitude of trunk and rural roads characterized by elevated risk levels and substantial traffic flows. These roads accommodate a diverse range of vehicles, including heavy trucks, cars, motorcycles, and nonmotorized vehicles, as well as pedestrians. The project was financed by a $200 million ADB loan, and a nearly equal amount of funding provided by the Shangnan county government and local transport agencies.

The Shaanxi Mountain Road Safety Demonstration Project incorporated engineered interventions to improve mountain road safety on more than 300 km of trunk and rural roads. The project incorporated roadside safety barriers, paved shoulders, realignments, and clearly marked pedestrian crossings on rural roads to reduce crashes in the Qinba Mountain Area in Shaanxi Province. The project included road safety training of provincial traffic management officers and engineers and

public information campaigns that sought to increase the use of seat belts and helmets, discourage speeding, and warn of the dangers of driving while fatigued or intoxicated. It also supported a community and road safety education program for schools in the project area, where teachers were trained to deliver road safety education.

The project was ADB's first stand-alone road safely demonstration project, and the first ADB-financed transport project in the PRC to use the International Road Assessment Programme (iRAP) for road safety inspection, road safety impact assessment, and design. The project was also the biggest stand-alone road safety project developed among multilateral development banks.

Star Ratings provide an objective measure of road safety risk as it relates to an individual road user (e.g., automobile passenger, bicyclist), based on dozens of road attributes. iRAP is a registered charity based in the United Kingdom that works to save lives by eliminating high-risk roads around the world, including in developing Asia.

The incorporation of iRAP Star Ratings into the project showed the benefits of road safety improvements to nontechnical stakeholders in and outside of government and demonstrated that hazardous road conditions could be mitigated through design interventions implemented with relatively minimal investment. It also helped in prioritizing different options, and in understanding the impacts of investments on safety. Stakeholders who do not usually

---

[7]   World Health Organization. 2018. Global Status Report on Road Safety 2018.

work together collaborated to deliver a solution—people and organizations in transport, law enforcement, education, and the community at large. Use of the tool was an integral part of the project's Safe System approach, which calls for transportation systems designed to accommodate human vulnerability and error in a way that reduces accidents.

Spreading Safety

Xiangtan. As a "demonstration" initiative, the Shaanxi Mountain Road Safety Project inspired the application of the iRAP methodology to ADB-financed projects in Xiangtan in the south-central part of the PRC. The Xiangtan Low-Carbon Transformation Sector Development Program, committed in 2020, is financed with a $200 million policy-based loan from ADB and $195.9 million in counterpart financing from the Xiangtan municipal government.

The investment aims to shift the focus of the local transportation system from being centered around cars to prioritizing mobility for people. Safety enhancements encompass raised crossings, curb extensions, abundant signage, and road markings designed to regulate speed and facilitate pedestrian crossings. An assessment conducted by an iRAP assessor evaluated road safety within school zones and suggested safety measures. The planned transformation of school zones at five primary schools intends to heighten awareness of road safety, achieving the criteria for achieving the highest safety rating for walking and cycling according to the iRAP Star Rating for Schools.

Knowledge sharing between ADB staff facilitated replication of iRAP methodology between the Shaanxi and Xiangtan projects. A team from iRAP presented their work in Shaanxi and on the efforts of the PRC's iRAP team to pilot improved safety around schools using the Star Rating for Schools program. Local stakeholders embraced the ideas because of the easy-to-understand approach with quantifiable outcomes.

Heilongjiang. In 2022, ADB committed a $193 million loan for the Heilongjiang Green Transformation Demonstration Project and Program. The loan is being complemented by government counterpart financing of $305.8 million. The project aims to adopt a systems approach to road safety like the one found in the Shaanxi project.

Road crash reduction program. Road safety features were implemented on 23 roads totaling about 478 kilometers under the Shaanxi Mountain Road Safety Project *(photo by the Project Management Office).*

Roads in Xunyang County. Major safety design enhancements were incorporated for roads under the Shaanxi Mountain Road Safety Project (*photo by the Project Management Office*).

During the design phase of the Heilongjiang project, local police flagged concerns related to road safety near schools. ADB helped to address these concerns by engaging ChinaRAP—the local chapter of iRAP—to perform road safety assessments using the iRAP Star Rating methodology. Based on an initial assessment, ChinaRAP developed a baseline Star Rating and a safer road investment plan identifying cost-effective safety countermeasures that, when incorporated into designs, would lead to the project roads achieving a target of 3 stars or better.

Replication is being nurtured through engagement of a behavior change consultant from Shaanxi Gender Development Solutions, a PRC-based nongovernment organization. The consultant, who worked on the road safety education component of the Shaanxi project, has designed a complementary education and public awareness campaign for the Heilongjiang project. The campaign should improve understanding of key road safety risk factors and safe behaviors around the schools where infrastructure improvements are planned.

Lessons from Replication

In each of these replication projects, the use of the Safe System approach was tailored to local needs and context. As was the case of the original project in Shaanxi, preparation of a needs assessment—including a baseline iRAP assessment—was the first step to address road safety issues. Further, in each instance, an investment plan allowed project stakeholders to see the costs and benefits of different options. The plan included measurable outcomes of different road safety interventions.

The involvement in the projects by an ADB staff member who communicated openly on road safety approaches and design was critical to effective adoption of successful features across interventions. Another factor contributing to replication was the positive contribution of iRAP's partnership officer in each of the projects approved after the Shaanxi project. The success of the project enabled replication beyond the PRC's borders (Box 3.1).

BOX 3.1
Moving Beyond the Borders of the People's Republic of China

Use of the International Road Assessment Programme (iRAP), applied in the Shaanxi Mountain Road Safety Demonstration Project in Shaanxi province in the People's Republic of China (PRC) did not stop at the country's borders. In 2019, the Asian Development Bank (ADB) committed a $2-million grant from the ADB-administered Japan Fund for Prosperous and Resilient Asia and the Pacific for Improving Transport Services in Ger Areas Project in Mongolia. The project reinforces an ongoing ADB-funded Ulaanbaatar Urban Services and Ger Areas Development Investment Program, a major intervention in the *ger* (tent) areas aimed at enhancing access to facilities and services. The project has also ameliorated the quality, accessibility, and safety of public transport services for *ger* area residents.

In preparing the *ger* areas project, ADB undertook a needs assessment. Part of the needs assessment was an initial iRAP study of the planned project's transportation corridor to identify a baseline. Key elements of the Safe System approach used in the Shaanxi project were introduced into the project. These include road safety audits for design and post-construction assessment, training for police officers, law enforcement, school education, and community awareness. ADB also went one step further and initiated communication with the police early in the process, recognizing that they are an important road safety stakeholder with views that could help shape improved project design. The police identified key behavioral risk factors and determined areas for police enforcement campaigns.

ADB provided two technical assistance (TA) projects to improve institutional capacities and develop a road safety policy and action plan in Mongolia. These TA projects laid the groundwork on the importance of a systems approach to road safety. Through these TA projects, government officials in Mongolia understood the benefit of adopting an approach that enabled the road safety outcomes of infrastructure improvements to be quantified. Another TA project managed by ADB's Nongovernment Organization and Civil Society Center engaged resource persons from the Global Road Safety Partnership of the International Federation of Red Cross and Red Crescent Societies and iRAP. They helped identify community needs and presented key road risks to Mongolian stakeholders. Lessons learned from other ADB-financed projects, including the Shaanxi Mountain Road Safety Demonstration Project, were shared.

Early results from the *ger* areas project are promising. All areas that were rated 1-star for pedestrians—the lowest rating on a 5-point scale—have been removed. The transportation corridor is likely to achieve a 3-star rating or better for pedestrians and vehicles. Data from police for 2023 showed a reduction in crashes involving serious injuries and fatalities in the project area.

Sources: ADB. 2018. *Technical Assistance Completion Report: Development of Road Safety Policy and Action Plan in Mongolia*; ADB. 2022. *Technical Assistance Completion Report: Institutional Strengthening for Road Safety in Mongolia*.

Catalyzing Finance for Energy Efficiency and Renewables

Situated in the northwestern region of the PRC, Shaanxi Province is a significant producer of coal, oil, and natural gas, with its industrial base heavily reliant on these fossil fuels. Although the province managed to reduce its energy intensity by 16.3% during the PRC's Twelfth Five-Year Plan (2011–2015) and decreased industrial energy intensity by 18.6% over the same period, these achievements primarily targeted large enterprises. The province set targets to augment the installed capacity of renewable energy from 7.5 gigawatts in 2015 to 20 gigawatts by 2020, aiming to diversify its electricity generation mix and generate approximately 19% of total electricity from renewable sources.

In Shaanxi Province, there are considerable untapped chances to lower energy intensity and curb air pollution stemming from small and medium-sized enterprises (SMEs), as these were not specifically addressed in the national Twelfth Five-Year Plan. Numerous SMEs in the province operate within energy-intensive sectors like coal-based chemicals, nonferrous metals, ceramic materials, building materials, and industrial waste recycling.

SMEs possess significant potential to lower their energy intensity and reduce air pollutants by recovering waste heat from industrial processes and utilizing industrial gases for productive purposes. However, their lack of awareness regarding such technologies, limited understanding of cost–benefit analysis, and challenges in obtaining commercial credit have hindered their ability to capitalize on these opportunities. Energy service companies, which include firms that implement energy efficiency projects financed through energy cost savings, are well-positioned to boost energy efficiency and technological advancements among SMEs. Yet energy service companies remain underdeveloped in Shaanxi and—like SMEs—find access to commercial credit more challenging than larger firms.

Commercial banks in the PRC hesitate to fund small-scale investments and SMEs are hesitant to use their limited assets as collateral for relatively minor energy efficiency investments. Moreover, securing assets related to energy efficiency is challenging because they are spread out and, while investments are small, they are technically intricate. In addition, banks lack familiarity with structuring cash flow-based, limited-recourse financing investments aimed at boosting energy efficiency.

ADB's Contribution to Clean Energy Financing

To reduce barriers confronted by energy service companies and SMEs seeking financing, ADB supported the province's launch of a clean energy financing platform. The platform was established under the Shaanxi Accelerated Energy Efficiency and Environmental Improvement Financing Project,[8] which was financed by a $150 million ADB loan and $309 million

---

8   ADB. 2016. *Report and Recommendation of the President to the Board of Directors: Proposed Loan to the People's Republic of China for the Shaanxi Accelerated Energy Efficiency and Environment Improvement Financing Project*; ADB. 2023. *Completion Report: Shaanxi Accelerated Energy Efficiency and Environment Improvement Financing Project in the People's Republic of China.*

in counterpart funding. It also supported initiatives designed to increase energy efficiency and reduce emissions.

Under the project, ADB and the provincial government forged partnerships with local commercial banks and financial institutions to direct funding resources to small or medium-scale clean energy investments. A financial intermediation loan modality was used since the financing requirements for the targeted investments were not large enough to warrant direct lending by ADB. The ADB loan attracted financing from participating commercial banks and other financial institutions, facilitating the funding of qualified energy efficiency investments on commercial terms.

The clean energy financing platform supported by the project introduced a debt financing mechanism to extend entrusted loans, a credit guarantee facility to enhance cofinancing opportunities, and a lease financing option for acquiring energy-efficient industrial equipment.

Collaborating with commercial banks in Shaanxi Province, the platform facilitated

entrusted loans, encouraging these banks to offer cofinancing equal to or exceeding the ADB loan amount. Moreover, the project's guarantee facility provided credit assurances to viable projects with substantial energy-saving prospects yet lacking adequate collateral to satisfy the cofinancing conditions set by commercial banks.

The clean energy financing platform supplemented the guarantees offered by Shaanxi SME Financing Guarantee Company, an executing agency partner, by depositing a cash amount equivalent to 20% (or less) of the guaranteed cofinancing loan into the beneficiary bank of the guarantee. This measure aimed to uphold a minimum leveraging ratio of five for the guarantee facility. In cases involving the acquisition of energy-efficient equipment, ADB loan funds could be allocated as lease financing through a financial leasing company.

By 2022, its clean energy financing platform had implemented nine energy conservation and emission reduction projects. According to preliminary estimates by third-party conservation assessment institutions, the Shaanxi Accelerated Energy Efficiency

Clean energy investments in Shaanxi Province. A geothermal heating technology project has been implemented in the Western China Science and Technology Innovation Harbor *(photo by Shaanxi Fengxi New Energy Development Company Ltd.).*

Energy-efficient cooling and heating. A comprehensive energy investment cooling and heating project is being implemented in Zhengdong New District of Henan Province *(photo by Shaanxi Fengxi New Energy Development Company Ltd.).*

and Environment Improvement Financing Project was expected to save 331,900 tons of standard coal and reduce CO_2 emissions by 919,000 tons by 2023.[9]

According to the Party Committee of Fengxi New City, Xixian New Area, the project at Innovation Harbor uses non-interference geothermal heating technology and medium-depth geothermal energy.[10] Utilizing a metal conduit and a heat exchange medium, heat (not water) is drawn from 2 to 3 km below surface level where it is possible to tap geothermal energy at temperatures ranging between 70°C and 120°C. The technology generates no pollution and is unaffected by the ground climate and other conditions—protecting groundwater resources while generating geothermal energy in an efficient and sustainable manner.

The Innovation Harbor project features six integrated energy supply stations that provide heating, cooling, and hot water for buildings with a total area of 1.59 million square meters. The project provides energy to thousands of researchers and faculty working at the Innovation Harbour campus of Xi'an Jiaotong University. Established in 1896, the elite educational institution is recognized as

a Double First-Class Construction University by the PRC's Ministry of Education.

Replication in Henan Province

A wholly owned Fengxi New City Energy Development Company subsidiary, Zhengzhou Zhengfeng Energy Development Co. Ltd. brought its techniques for harnessing geothermal energy from the Shaanxi project to two replicated projects in Zhengzhou, the capital of Henan Province.

One of the replicated projects is the Comprehensive Energy Investment and Cooling and Heating Project of Zhengdong New District Science Valley Digital Town (Phase 1). This project is under construction, with a budget of CNY350 million (about $48 million). Once completed, it will provide clean energy cooling and heating for the Software Town project of the Zhengdong New District. The project is expected to eliminate the need for 13,000 tons of standard coal and reduce CO_2 emissions by 38,000 tons annually.

Non-interference geothermal technology is also used in the other project replicated in Zhendong by Zhengzhou Zhengfeng

[9]   ADB. 2023. Asia Clean Energy Forum: Navigating toward a Carbon-Neutral Future through Clean Energy Solutions. 13–16 June.
[10] A. Richter. 2019. City In Shaanxi Province, China Launches Innovative Large-Scale Geothermal District Heating System. *Think Geoenergy*. 19 December.

Harnessing geothermal energy. Project site in Zhengdong New District *(photo by Shaanxi Fengxi New Energy Development Company Ltd.)*.

Energy Development Co. Ltd. This project will provide heating for the Yunxiyuan and Fengqiyuan residential quarters in the Baisha area of Zhengdong New District. When operational, it is expected to feature about 16 non-interference geothermal wells, a piping network, and a pair of heating stations. A total of CNY60 million (about $8.2 million) is being mobilized for the project. Compared with the traditional coal-fired heating method, the project could replace about 2,500 tons of coal in a heating season and reduce CO_2 emissions by about 6,700 tons annually.

A Powerful Demonstration Effect

The Shaanxi Accelerated Energy Efficiency and Environment Improvement Financing Project has contributed to reduced energy intensity and emissions in Shaanxi Province, which has continued to expand the share of its power needs provided by renewable sources. Importantly, the project has reduced the financing barriers to clean energy investments in the province, and, by 2023, leveraged the equivalent of $1.73 billion for clean energy investments.[11] Significantly, techniques for harnessing geothermal energy used in the Shaanxi project were replicated by a state-owned enterprise in two other non-ADB-financed projects in Zhengzhou, Henan Province.

The PRC plays a pivotal role in shaping Asia's energy landscape. Its pursuit of energy efficiency and development of renewable energy sources are driving technological innovation, stimulating job creation, and further cementing the PRC's place as a global leader in green technologies. Through cooperation with other developing Asian countries, the PRC can catalyze a region-wide transformation toward sustainable energy use, setting the stage for a more prosperous and environmentally conscious future.

---

[11] ADB. 2023. *Completion Report: Shaanxi Accelerated Energy Efficiency and Environment Improvement Financing Project in the People's Republic of China.*

Improving the Urban Environment Through Integrated Water Resources Management

Wuhan is 1 of the 10 most populous cities in the PRC, and capital of Hubei Province. About a quarter of the urban area is made up of lakes and rivers, which form an intricate water system within the expansive Jianghan flood plain. Wuhan's two existing wastewater treatment plants that were in operation as of 2000 were only able to treat 6% of the urban area's wastewater.

Untreated wastewater flowing directly into lakes and rivers negatively impacted Wuhan's water quality. More than half of the rivers and nearly 90% of the lakes were polluted by various wastes. Because Wuhan is in a subtropical monsoon climate zone, heavy summer rains would put great stress on the dated urban drainage network. The city often experienced severe flooding, and sewer overflows became a significant source of water pollution. However, by 2008, about 80% of Wuhan's wastewater was treated following two loans from ADB.[12] Nevertheless, the city continued to cope with growing amounts of sewage sludge generated by wastewater treatment plants serving a large and growing population.

ADB Support for Sewage and Wastewater Treatment in Wuhan

The Wuhan Urban Environmental Improvement Project was formulated to address this major environmental issue. The project provided financial resources and applied know-how to water resource management and wastewater sludge treatment and disposal in Wuhan city between 2010 and 2020. An ADB loan financed $98.1 million of the $501.8 million total project cost.

The loan supported construction of facilities to treat sludge from five of Wuhan's wastewater treatment plants, most of which were built with the support of previous ADB loans. The sludge treatment plants contributed to a sustainable, integrated concept of urban development. The project supported sludge digestion, improved the performance of wastewater treatment plants, and reduced pressure on landfills, which had served as the primary means of sludge disposal.

The project built a flood pumping station of 105 cubic meters (m³) per second, dredged 16 km of channels, and enlarged the lake retention capacity by 1 million m³ through sludge dredging. At the same time, the project established an intelligent integrated watershed management system to monitor water quality and the watershed flood. These measures have strengthened the city's flood management capacity. Further, the project supported the rehabilitation of Yangchun

---

[12] ADB. 2003. *Report and Recommendation of the President to the Board of Directors: Proposed Loan to the People's Republic of China for the Wuhan Wastewater Management Project*; ADB. 2006. *Report and Recommendation of the President to the Board of Directors: Proposed Loan to the People's Republic of China for the Wuhan Wastewater and Stormwater Management Project.*

Lake through the recovery of the lake's surface, ecological treatment, greening, and construction of an artificial wetland.

By 2018, 100% of the total sludge being produced by Wuhan's wastewater treatment plants was being treated and reused as planting soil, cement-plant material, building material, and power-plant comburent, contributing to sustainable urban development, which extended the life of the city's landfills.

In addition, the project brought down sludge-transport costs, reduced greenhouse gas emissions, and strengthened water system resilience. Ultimately, it contributed to the development of a comprehensive approach to managing water resources that considers the interactions between various surface water systems, such as rivers and lakes, as well as their connections with groundwater and other natural processes.

Informing Urban Environmental Management in Huangshi and Huainan

The benefits of this ADB intervention were not limited to Wuhan city, as lessons learned from the project fed into the design and implementation of subsequent ADB-financed water and urban infrastructure projects in Hubei Province, including the Hubei Huangshi Urban Pollution Control and Environment Management Project. Replication of project features was supported by knowledge-sharing among staff of ADB and external experts. It was also aided by ADB's ongoing dialogue with authorities in Hubei Province and government initiatives to promote healthy and environmentally sustainable cities.

Huangshi city is spread over a floodplain on the south bank of the Yangtze River, about 80 km southeast of Wuhan. The city's

Lake rehabilitation. ADB supported the recovery of lake surface, ecological treatment, and greening of Yangchun Lake, and construction of a stormwater treatment system and artificial wetland (*photo by Zhimin Xie, Wuhan Project Management Office*).

Integrating pollution control and ecological rehabilitation. ADB helped improved the water quality of Cihu Lake, providing healthy conditions for the residents (*photo by Yongqin Xiong, Huangshi Project Management Office*).

economic development has relied heavily on mining and related industries. The municipal government decided that it would be in the best interests of the city to pursue more balanced and sustainable development through an urban renewal strategy.

Huangshi's longstanding dependence on heavy industry and underinvestment in urban infrastructure have created problems. The dumping of untreated industrial and domestic wastewater into the city's main lakes led to serious water pollution problems. Sludge from wastewater treatment plants was untreated. Public health and safety of people residing in the vicinity of polluted inland waterways became endangered.

In 2012, ADB approved the Hubei Huangshi Urban Pollution Control and Environmental Management Project. It was partially financed with a $100 million ADB loan that was used to support improvements in urban environmental infrastructure and services. The project embraced an integrated approach that included sludge treatment, wastewater collection and treatment, lake rehabilitation, and construction of urban wetlands as in the Wuhan Urban Environmental Improvement Project.

Sludge treatment facilities built by the Hubei Huangshi project had the capacity to process 179 tons of sludge per day. Some of the treated sludge was then used as a raw material in cement production, emulating the example set by the Wuhan project. The treatment of sludge extended the service life of existing landfill facilities. The project also constructed a wastewater treatment plant; installed nearly 80 km of sewers; constructed three pumping stations; and procured sewer maintenance equipment, monitoring devices, and vehicles.

Sludge was dredged and construction was carried out to create permeable roads, a recessed garden, trenches, and embankments. About 1.25 million m³ of contaminated sediments were removed from Cihu, Qingshan, and Qinggang lakes in the city. Treated wastewater discharged from the wastewater treatment plant (80,000 m³ per day) was reused and further treated by newly constructed wetlands with an area of 115.8 ha.

The Hubei Huangshi project also introduced improvements to solid waste collection and transfer stations and set up a community solid waste sorting scheme. This scheme, together with community-based solid waste recycling, was later incorporated in the city's action plan on municipal solid waste sorting management in 2022.

The project contributed to Huangshi's gradual transformation from a city best known for mining and heavy industry to a sustainable urban area attractive to tourists. Real estate projects have been attracted to the wetland area and rehabilitated areas around Cihu, Qingshan, and Qinggang lakes. Water quality has steadily improved so much so that swans, which were absent for more than a decade, have returned to Cihu lake since 2022. People also began to return to homes along the wetland as living conditions improved.

Experience from the Wuhan Urban Environmental Improvement Project also informed the Anhui Huainan Urban Water Systems Integrated Rehabilitation Project in neighboring Anhui Province. The Huainan municipality has been known for its coal industry and thermal power plants but seeks to develop a greener image. The ADB project, approved in 2013, drew upon lessons related to flood control and environment improvement found in the Wuhan project. ADB has funded the Huainan project through a $150 million loan, which is being complemented by $193.3 million in government counterpart funding.

As in the case of Hubei Huangshi project, replication from the project in Wuhan was facilitated by knowledge-sharing within ADB's East Asia Department, ongoing dialogue with subnational authorities, and alignment with government policies and plans, as well as the ADB–PRC country partnership strategy. The Huainan municipal government requested ADB funding to support its master plan (2010–2020), which aimed to enhance the quality of urban water systems to at least Class IV, and to create a system designed to manage storm waters and handle a once-in-2-decades weather event.

The Anhui Huianan project is improving wastewater collection facilities. It is also connecting more than 3,000 households to new sewers, and shifting 5,700 other households from existing combined sewers to new sewers. Wastewater treatment rates are expected to increase from 64% to 80% in the urban area.

Drawing on the experience from the community participation in the solid waste sorting scheme of the Hubei Huangshi project, this project is piloting

Positive environmental impact. Swans, which were absent for more than a decade, reappear in Cihu lake following improvement in water quality (*photo by Yongqin Xiong, Huangshi Project Management Office*).

Clean urban environment. Wetland construction improved water quality, making Huangshi city more environmentally friendly and livable (*photo by Yongqin Xiong, Huangshi Project Management Office*).

community-based environmental supervision and flood management teams. There are also plans to introduce improved water and environmental monitoring of urban water channels and build the capacity of personnel in the Huainan municipal government to carry out maintenance functions. Several environmental supervision and flood management teams have been established in local areas seriously affected by pollution and floods. In addition, they have heightened community awareness about the risks of dumping wastes into urban water channels and how the flood warning system operates.

Like the Wuhan and Hubei Huangshi projects, the Anhui Huainan project is protecting urban lakes from pollution. Artificial wetlands have been constructed at major discharge points into four lakes. An urban water quality and ecological monitoring system was established to monitor water quality and strengthen the capacity and management of the municipal government. It is anticipated that the project will lower the risks of flooding while upgrading the water environment for nearly 1 million urban residents of Huainan.

Conclusion

The Wuhan Urban Environmental Improvement Project's innovative design and effective implementation created valuable demonstration effects. It was the first ADB-financed operation in the PRC to support comprehensive sludge management while promoting the circular economy. Beneficiary use of sludge promoted by the project provided a model for handling treated sludge, extending the operational life of landfills, lowering sludge-transportation costs, and reducing greenhouse gas emissions, among other environmental benefits. Further, it has served as an excellent model for urban lake rehabilitation, flood management, and integrated surface water management for other jurisdictions in Hubei Province and elsewhere in the country.

▶ Conclusion

Replication starts with the demonstration of an idea, technology, or way of doing things that generates a positive impact and can be applied in the same or adapted fashion to another context. ADB's experience in the PRC shows that this process is more likely where there is active knowledge exchange, strong government support, significant value added, and official recognition. Replication receives a boost when projects align closely with government plans and strategies and when ADB proactively transfers learnings from one project to another.

From within the country, knowledge gained from the Wuhan environmental improvement flowed over to Hubei and Anhui, improving the overall quality of life of the people within these provinces; knowledge on energy efficiency initiatives from Shaanxi Province are being transferred to Henan Province. Meanwhile, the application of lessons gained from some projects exceeded the geographical boundaries of the PRC. For example, biodiversity efforts in Jiangsu Province have given rise to the East Asian–Australasian Flyway, a regional initiative. Road safety initiatives generated through a road safety project in northwestern PRC have saved thousands of lives when cascaded to other PRC provinces and Mongolia. Likewise, green development funds, initiated in Shandong Province, have now found their way to Southeast Asia and Central and West Asia—supporting efforts toward green finance.

The partnership between ADB and the PRC has centered on the generation of knowledge, given the PRC's rich experiences, to promote green and sustainable development such as in the areas of biodiversity protection, green finance, road safety, and renewable energy. Its strong institutional and project implementation capacities make it ideal for piloting new development approaches.

ADB and the PRC can further collaborate to encourage knowledge sharing on innovative practices among central and subnational authorities, project implementation units, and implementing agencies. Other knowledge-sharing platforms include high-level forums in various sectors organized by ADB, the National Development and Reform Commission and other PRC line ministries, and other development partners. In addition, the Regional Knowledge Sharing Initiative, launched by ADB and the Government of the PRC, continues to provide a structured framework for ADB and the government to organize knowledge-sharing events, including the annual East Asia Forum.

Protecting the environment and enhancing biodiversity, investing in green economy, and preparing for energy efficiency are all common aims toward a sustainable future.

Ultimately, the replication of ADB-financed projects in the PRC in these areas can help accelerate progress toward achieving sustainable development goals, benefiting millions of people across the PRC and other countries in Asia and the Pacific.

www.ingramcontent.com/pod-product-compliance
Lightning Source LLC
Chambersburg PA
CBHW041122280326

41928CB00061B/3494